BARK

BARK

Selected Poems About Dogs

Illustrations by Ferris Cook

A Bulfinch Press Book
Little, Brown and Company
Boston · New York · London

Also available with illustrations by Ferris Cook

A Murmur in the Trees / Emily Dickinson
Odes to Common Things / Pablo Neruda
Odes to Opposites / Pablo Neruda
The Rose Window and Other Verse from New Poems / Rainer Maria Rilke
The Sonnets / William Shakespeare

First Edition

ISBN: 0-8212-2664-9
Library of Congress Control Number: 00-103334

Bulfinch Press is an imprint and trademark of
Little, Brown and Company (Inc.)

Printed in the United States of America

For Sarah and Sparky

A dog barks in rhyme but the rhyme is never planned by the dog. This is not a value judgment in any way but it may be an introduction to the consideration of the aesthetic pleasures of being and not being a dog.

—Kenneth Koch, from "My Olivetti Speaks"

CONTENTS

BARK

VERSE FOR A CERTAIN DOG

Such glorious faith as fills your limpid eyes,
    Dear little friend of mine, I never knew.
All-innocent are you, and yet all-wise.
    (For Heaven's sake, stop worrying that shoe!)
You look about, and all you see is fair;
    This mighty globe was made for you alone.
Of all the thunderous ages, you're the heir.
    (Get off the pillow with that dirty bone!)

A skeptic world you face with steady gaze;
    High in young pride you hold your noble head;
Gayly you meet the rush of roaring days.
    (*Must* you eat puppy biscuit on the bed?)
Lancelike your courage, gleaming swift and strong,
    Yours the white rapture of a wingèd soul,
Yours is a spirit like a May-day song.
    (God help you, if you break the goldfish bowl!)

"Whatever is, is good" — your gracious creed.
    You wear your joy of living like a crown.
Love lights your simplest act, your every deed.
    (Drop it, I tell you — put that kitten down!)
You are God's kindliest gift of all — a friend.
    Your shining loyalty unflecked by doubt,
You ask but leave to follow to the end.
    (Couldn't you wait until I took you out?)

                       —*Dorothy Parker*

DACHSHUNDS

The deer and the dachshund are one.
—Wallace Stevens, "Loneliness in Jersey City"

The Dachshund leads a quiet life
    Not far above the ground;
He takes an elongated wife,
    They travel all around.

They leave the lighted metropole;
    Nor turn to look behind
Upon the headlands of the soul,
    The tundras of the mind.

They climb together through the dusk
    To ask the Lost-and-Found
For information on the stars
    Not far above the ground.

The Dachshunds seem to journey on:
    And following them, I
Take up my monocle, the Moon,
    And gaze into the sky.

Pursuing them with comic art
    Beyond a cosmic goal,
I see the whole within the part,
    The part within the whole;

See planets wheeling overhead,
   Mysterious and slow,
While Morning buckles on his red,
   And on the Dachshunds go.

—William Jay Smith

THE SPAN OF LIFE

The old dog barks backward without getting up.
I can remember when he was a pup.

—*Robert Frost*

IF FEELING ISN'T IN IT

You can take it away, as far as I'm concerned — I'd rather
spend the afternoon with a nice dog. I'm not kidding. Dogs
have what a lot of poems lack: excitements and responses,
a sense of play, the ability to impart warmth, elation. . . .

—Howard Moss

Dogs will also lick your face if you let them.
Their bodies will shiver with happiness.
A simple walk in the park is just about
the height of contentment for them, followed
by a bowl of food, a bowl of water,
a place to curl up and sleep. Someone
to scratch them where they can't reach
and smooth their foreheads and talk to them.
Dogs also have a natural dislike of mailmen
and other bringers of bad news and will
bite them on your behalf. Dogs can smell
fear and also love with perfect accuracy.
There is no use pretending with them.
Nor do they pretend. If a dog is happy
or sad or nervous or bored or ashamed
or sunk in contemplation, everybody knows it.
They make no secret of themselves.
You can even tell what they're dreaming about

by the way their legs jerk and try to run
on the slippery ground of sleep.
Nor are they given to pretentious self-importance.
They don't try to impress you with how serious
or sensitive they are. They just feel everything
full blast. Everything is off the charts
with them. More than once I've seen a dog
waiting for its owner outside a café
practically *implode* with worry. "Oh, God,
what if she doesn't come back this time?
What will I do? Who will take care of me?
I loved her so much and now she's gone
and I'm tied to a post surrounded by people
who don't look or smell or sound like her at all."
And when she does come, what a flurry
of commotion, what a chorus of yelping
and cooing and leaps straight up into the air!
It's almost unbearable, this sudden
fullness after such total loss, to see
the world made whole again by a hand
on the shoulder and a voice like no other.

—*John Brehm*

POOR ROVER

Rover was in clover
With a bone
On the front lawn —
But Rover's fun was over
When his bone
Was gone.
Poor Rover!

—Langston Hughes

ODE TO THE DOG

The dog is asking me a question
and I have no answer.
He dashes through the countryside and asks me
wordlessly,
and his eyes
are two moist question marks, two wet
inquiring flames,
but I do not answer
because I haven't got the answer.
I have nothing to say.

Dog and man: together we roam
the open countryside.

Leaves shine as
if someone
had kissed them
one by one,
orange trees
rise up from the earth
raising
minute planetariums
in trees that are as rounded
and green as the night,
while we roam together, dog and man
sniffing everything, jostling clover
in the countryside of Chile,
cradled by the bright fingers of September.
The dog makes stops,
chases bees,
leaps over restless water,
listens to far-off
barking,
pees on a rock,
and presents me the tip of his snout
as if it were a gift:

it is the freshness of his love,
his message of love.
And he asks me
with both eyes:
why is it daytime? why does night always fall?
why does spring bring
nothing
in its basket
for wandering dogs
but useless flowers,
flowers and more flowers?
This is how the dog
asks questions
and I do not reply.

Together we roam,
man and dog bound together again
by the bright green morning,
by the provocative empty solitude
in which we alone
exist,
this union of dog and dew
or poet and woods.
For these two companions,

for these fellow-hunters,
there is no lurking fowl
or secret berry
but only birdsong and sweet smells,
a world moistened
by night's distillations,
a green tunnel and then
a meadow,
a gust of orangey air,
the murmurings of roots,
life on the move,
breathing and growing,
and the ancient friendship,
the joy
of being dog or being man
fused
in a single beast
that pads along on
six feet,
wagging
its dew-wet tail.

—*Pablo Neruda*

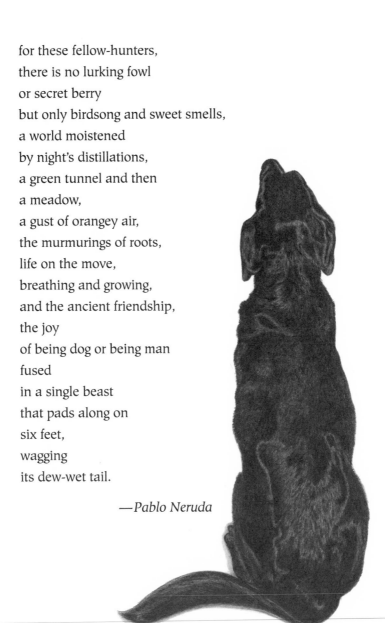

CLANCY THE DOG

—for Claire

He is so ugly he is a psalm to ugliness,
this extraterrestrial, shorthaired
midget sea lion,
snorts, farts, grunts, turns somersaults
on his mistress's bed.

She calls him an imperfect Boston terrier,
part gnome, part elf,
half something and half something else,
180,000,000-year-old Clancy
with his yellowy-white, pin-pointy teeth
and red, misshapen prehistoric gums.

Clancy has no tail at all and doesn't bark.
He squeaks like a monkey,
flies through the air,
lands at six every morning
on his mistress's head,
begging to be fed and wrapped not in a robe
but a spread.

Tree frog, warthog, groundhog,
"Clancy, Clancy," she calls for him
in the early morning fog,
and he appears, anything, anything,
part anything but a dog.

—*Robert Sward*

86

The dog hangs his snout
                    out the auto window
Too long city-pent
                his nose is out for wild game
His tongue hangs out
                    when he gets the scent
            of small creatures in the underbrush
        for whom every car is a brush
                            with disaster
And the dog feels for them
                    with his so sad eyes
        but looks at them
                    through the eyes of his master

                            —*Lawrence Ferlinghetti*

DOG'S DEATH

She must have been kicked unseen or brushed by a car.
Too young to know much, she was beginning to learn
To use the newspapers spread on the kitchen floor
And to win, wetting there, the words, "Good dog! Good dog!"

We thought her shy malaise was a shot reaction.
The autopsy disclosed a rupture in her liver.
As we teased her with play, blood was filling her skin
And her heart was learning to lie down forever.

Monday morning, as the children were noisily fed
And sent to school, she crawled beneath the youngest's bed.
We found her twisted and limp but still alive.
In the car to the vet's, on my lap, she tried

To bite my hand and died. I stroked her warm fur
And my wife called in a voice imperious with tears.
Though surrounded by love that would have upheld her,
Nevertheless she sank and, stiffening, disappeared.

Back home, we found that in the night her frame,
Drawing near to dissolution, had endured the shame
Of diarrhoea and had dragged across the floor
To a newspaper carelessly left there. *Good dog.*

—John Updike

PINKS

Pinks is this dog's name,
she stinks all the same.

In neither hill nor dale
is there a sweeter flower:
in height she may not tower,
but her stench tells quite a tale.
Let us praise Pinks without fail,
raising our noses to her fame!
Pinks is this dog's name,
she stinks all the same.

May God forgive the one
who gave her the name of Pinks.
You know how bad she stinks:
couldn't we call her Gun?
Shooting pellets one by one
is how she plays her game.
Pinks is this dog's name,
she stinks all the same.

It's not hard to surmise
that, if eyesight serves us well,
other pinks' buds have the smell,
while this one smells to the eyes.
Surely she must take the prize

for Most Aromatic dame.
Pinks is this dog's name,
she stinks all the same.

—*Luis de Góngora*

THE GIFT

Lord, You may not recognize me
speaking for someone else.
I have a son. He is
so little, so ignorant.
He likes to stand
at the screen door, calling
oggie, oggie, entering
language, and sometimes
a dog will stop and come up
the walk, perhaps
accidentally. May he believe
this is not an accident?
At the screen
welcoming each beast
in love's name, Your emissary.

—*Louise Glück*

WHAT THE DOG PERHAPS HEARS

If an inaudible whistle
blown between our lips
can send him home to us,
then silence is perhaps
the sound of spiders breathing
and roots mining the earth;
it may be asparagus heaving,
headfirst, into the light
and the long brown sound
of cracked cups, when it happens.
We would like to ask the dog
if there is a continuous whir
because the child in the house
keeps growing, if the snake
really stretches full length
without a click and the sun
breaks through the clouds without
a decibel of effort;
whether in autumn, when the trees
dry up their wells, there isn't a shudder
too high for us to hear.

What is it like up there
above the shut-off level
of our simple ears?
For us there was no birth-cry,

the newborn bird is suddenly here,
the egg broken, the nest alive,
and we heard nothing when the world changed.

—*Lisel Mueller*

DOG

Howl after pitiful, aching howl: an enormous, efficiently muscular
       doberman pinscher
has trapped itself in an old-fashioned phone booth, the door closed
       firmly upon it,
but when someone approaches to try to release it, the howl quickens
       and descends,

and if someone in pity dares anyway lean on and crack open an inch
       the obstinate hinge,
the quickened howl is a snarl, the snarl a blade lathed in the scarlet
       gape of the gullet,
and the creature powers itself towards that sinister slit, ears
       flattened, fangs flashing,

the way, caught in the deepest, most unknowing cell of itself, heart's
       secret, heart's wound,
decorous usually, seemly, though starving now, desperate, will turn
       nonetheless, raging,
ready to kill, or die, to stay where it is, to maintain itself just as it is,
       decorous, seemly.

—C. K. Williams

1989

Because AIDS was slaughtering people left and right,
    I went to a lot of memorial services that year.
There were so many, I'd pencil them in between
    a movie or a sale at Macy's. The other thing that
made them tolerable was the funny stories people
    got up and told about the deceased: the time he
hurled a mushroom frittata across a crowded room,
    those green huaraches he refused to throw away,
the joke about the flight attendant and the banana
    that cracked him up every time.

But this funeral was for a blind friend of my wife's
    who'd merely died. And the interesting thing
about it was the guide dogs; with all the harness
    and the sniffing around, the vestibule of the church
looked like the starting line of the Iditarod. But
    nobody got up to talk. We just sat there
and the pastor read the King James version. Then he
    said someday we would see Robert and he us.

Throughout the service, the dogs slumped beside their
    masters. But when the soloist stood and launched
into a screechy rendition of "Abide with Me," they sank
    into the carpet. A few put their paws over their ears.
Someone whispered to one of the blind guys; he told
    another, and the laughter started to spread. People

in the back looked around, startled and embarrassed,
    until they spotted all those chunky Labradors
flattened out like animals in a cartoon about
    steamrollers. Then they started, too.

That was more like it. That was what I was used to —
    a roomful of people laughing and crying, taking off
their sunglasses to blot their inconsolable eyes.

—*Ron Koertge*

WALKING THE DOG

Two universes mosey down the street
Connected by love and a leash and nothing else.
Mostly I look at lamplight through the leaves
While he mooches along with tail up and snout down,
Getting a secret knowledge through the nose
Almost entirely hidden from my sight.

We stand while he's enraptured by a bush
Till I can't stand our standing any more
And haul him off; for our relationship
Is patience balancing to this side tug
And that side drag; a pair of symbionts
Contented not to think each other's thoughts.

What else we have in common's what he taught,
Our interest in shit. We know its every state
From steaming fresh through stink to nature's way
Of sluicing it downstreet dissolved in rain
Or drying it to dust that blows away.
We move along the street inspecting shit.

His sense of it is keener far than mine,
And only when he finds the place precise
He signifies by sniffing urgently
And circles thrice about, and squats, and shits,
Whereon we both with dignity walk home
And just to show who's master I write the poem.

—*Howard Nemerov*

33

ANOTHER REASON WHY I DON'T KEEP A GUN IN THE HOUSE

The neighbors' dog will not stop barking.
He is barking the same high, rhythmic bark
that he barks every time they leave the house.
They must switch him on on their way out.

The neighbors' dog will not stop barking.
I close all the windows in the house
and put on a Beethoven symphony full blast
but I can still hear him muffled under the music,
barking, barking, barking,

and now I can see him sitting in the orchestra,
his head raised confidently as if Beethoven
had included a part for barking dog.

When the record finally ends he is still barking,
sitting there in the oboe section barking,
his eyes fixed on the conductor who is
entreating him with his baton

while the other musicians listen in respectful
silence to the famous barking dog solo,
that endless coda that first established
Beethoven as an innovative genius.

—*Billy Collins*

BARK WITH AUTHORITY

I tell my dog, bête noire of the backyard,
unbellicose beast, he with the musculature
of a canine warrior, all beef and brawn;
bark with Byzantine glory, with bravura,
bark with the rumblings of ruptured nerve:
be brazen and boisterous, be jowled in howls,
be loose in the lungs, a grounded leviathan;
be blue in the throat from sounding an alarm.
Rip your voice through the dazzle of the rich,
through the daze of the poor, through storm
and drought, through the whines of Boy Scouts
out on their hike, through coyote's whistle;
rouse your ruff to a roar that ripples
the air like a serrated knife, that riots
in the ear until the world shouts Stop!
But you, sad Sam, named for the word-man
who barked out a lexicon of rapturous sounds,
you with your doleful eyes, crooked smile,
with your quizzical gaze, your velvet snout:
you shrug your shoulders, tune me out,
would rather stand shyly behind old Molly,
your surrogate dam, that grizzled old bitch,
arthritic and wobbly, though still wily —
you'd rather demur to her dominance, yes?
Well, what's it to me if you'd prefer modesty,

being the foil, the sidekick, Laurel to Hardy?
What do I care if you live out your days,
indeed your dog days, without doggerel or dog-
eared memories, with a dogged suspicion, dog-
faced and dog-headed and -hearted, that you've
gone, dog-gone it, to the dogs, so to speak,
and that your only dogma, your only dog's letter
(trilled in your sleep when you're dog-tired)
that weathers your lips begins with an "S" —
and ushers in snoozing and supper and silence?

—Maurya Simon

SPRING

I lift my face to the pale flowers
of the rain. They're soft as linen,
clean as holy water. Meanwhile
my dog runs off, noses down packed leaves
into damp, mysterious tunnels.
He says the smells are rising now
stiff and lively; he says the beasts
are waking up now full of oil,
sleep sweat, tag-ends of dreams. The rain
rubs its shining hands all over me.
My dog returns and barks fiercely, he says
each secret body is the richest advisor,
deep in the black earth such fuming
nuggets of joy!

—*Mary Oliver*

DOG MUSIC

Amongst dogs are listeners and singers.
My big dog sang with me so purely,
puckering her ruffled lips into an O,
beginning with small, swallowing sounds
like Coltrane musing, then rising to power
and resonance, gulping air to continue —
her passion and sense of flawless form —
singing not with me, but for the art of dogs.
We joined in many fine songs — "Stardust,"
"Naima," "The Trout," "My Rosary," "Perdido."
She was a great master and died young,
leaving me with unrelieved grief,
her talents known to only a few.

Now I have a small dog who does not sing,
but listens with discernment, requiring
skill and spirit in my falsetto voice.
I sing her name and words of love
andante, con brio, vivace, adagio.
Sometimes she is so moved she turns
to place a paw across her snout,
closes her eyes, sighing like a girl
I held and danced with years ago.

But I am a pretender to dog music.
The true strains rise only from
the rich, red chambers of a canine heart,
these melodies best when the moon is up,
listeners and singers together or
apart, beyond friendship and anger,
far from any human imposter—
ballads of long nights lifting
to starlight, songs of bones, turds,
conquests, hunts, smells, rankings,
things settled long before our birth.

—*Paul Zimmer*

OLD DOG QUEENIE

Old Dog Queenie
Was such a meanie,
She spent her life
Barking at the scenery.

—Langston Hughes

KILTY SUE

Instincts jammed by lack of sheep
in this region, she attends to babies, ducklings —
anything small and in need of care.
A border collie whose eyes, opposite
shades of brown, offer the look
of a slightly retarded devil-dog. And,
if you must know, she bites people:
my brother, presumably, because he was mean
to me at a younger age; the UPS man
because he carries a package too quickly towards
my pregnant sister; my mother-in-law, I suppose,
to keep in shape. And various relatives
and strangers — Kilty Sue reminds them
of the precise location of their Achilles' tendon.
Mind you, she never actually rips it out,
but merely offers a sharp touch. Like a pin-prick,
only deeper, her bites spring out
from a sudden vortex of silence. When Kilty Sue howls —
in a voice high and piercing as a drunken soprano,
and you wish your ears would just drop off and die —
you are safe. She is protecting you.

—*Marck Beggs*

FALLING DOG

I am lying on a giant dead sequoia.
I hear something at the top of the cliff,
among the stinging nettles and the madrona.
I open my eyes and see the sand wall
cave in, see the swallows' nests and lovers' names
disappear. A dog, a strong dark mongrel,
falls fifty feet through the air, his body
bouncing off this ancient tree with a thud.
I watch him, a moment, motionless on the sand.
I place my hand on his still rib cage.
His chest begins to rise and fall.
He stands, shakes once, hard, all over,
runs down the beach as if nothing had happened.
In one animal motion he shrugged off the pain . . .
No, the numbness from being uprooted . . .
What has taken me seventeen years,
an inch or so measured in this dead tree's rings.

—*Michael Moos*

TO A FOOLISH DOG

Joxer, bouncing harlequin,
All ingratiating grin,
Which begat thee, jolly Joxer?
Airedale, poodle, beagle, boxer?
Scottie braw or Irish terrier?
Never mind, the more the merrier;
A pedigree so heterodox
Perks up thy personality, Jox,
For thou, rambunctious residual,
Wert whelped unique and individual,
A blithe buffoon, a jester pampered,
Nor by the *Ten* Commandments hampered
(I know thou triflest with the Seventh),
But Joxer, mind the stern Eleventh,
Or learn from choking leash and baffling tether
Thy neighbor's Leghorns thou shalt not de-feather.

—*Ogden Nash*

TRIBUTE TO THE MEMORY OF THE SAME DOG

Lie here, without a record of thy worth,
Beneath a covering of the common earth!
It is not from unwillingness to praise,
Or want of love, that here no Stone we raise;
More thou deserv'st; but *this* man gives to man,
Brother to brother, this is all we can.
Yet they to whom thy virtues made thee dear
Shall find thee through all changes of the year:
This Oak points out thy grave; the silent tree
Will gladly stand a monument of thee.

We grieved for thee, and wished thy end were past;
And willingly have laid thee here at last:
For thou hadst lived, till every thing that cheers
In thee had yielded to the weight of years;
Extreme old age had wasted thee away,
And left thee but a glimmering of the day;
Thy ears were deaf, and feeble were thy knees, —
I saw thee stagger in the summer breeze,
Too weak to stand against its sportive breath,
And ready for the gentlest stroke of death.
It came, and we were glad; yet tears were shed;
Both man and woman wept when thou wert dead;
Not only for a thousand thoughts that were,
Old household thoughts, in which thou hadst thy share;

But for some precious boons vouchsafed to thee,
Found scarcely anywhere in like degree!
For love, that comes wherever life and sense
Are given by God, in thee was most intense;
A chain of heart, a feeling of the mind,
A tender sympathy, which did thee bind
Not only to us Men, but to thy Kind:
Yea, for thy fellow-brutes in thee we saw
A soul of love, love's intellectual law: —
Hence, if we wept, it was not done in shame;
Our tears from passion and from reason came,
And, therefore, shalt thou be an honoured name!

—*William Wordsworth*

CUSTODIAN

Every spring when the ice goes out
black commas come scribbling across the shallows.
Soon they sprout forelegs.
Slowly they absorb their tails
and by mid-June, full-voiced, announce themselves.

Enter our spotted dog.
Every summer, tense with the scent of them,
tail arced like a pointer's but wagging
in anticipation, he stalks his frogs
two hundred yards clockwise around
the perimeter of this mucky pond,
then counterclockwise, an old pensioner
happy in his work.

Once every ten or so pounces
he succeeds, carries his captive north
in his soft mouth, uncorks him on the grass,
and then sits, head cocked, watching the slightly
dazed amphibian hop back to sanctuary.

Over the years the pond's inhabitants
seem to have grown accustomed
to this ritual of capture and release.
They ride untroubled in the wet pocket
of the dog's mouth, disembark in the meadow
like hitchhikers, and strike out again for home.

I have seen others of his species kill
and swallow their catch and then be seized
with violent retchings. I have seen children
corner polliwogs in the sun-flecked hollow
by the green rock and lovingly squeeze
the life out of them in their small fists.
I have seen the great blue heron swoop in
time after wing-slapping time to carry
frogs back to the fledglings in the rookery.

Nothing is to be said here
of need or desire. No moral arises
nor is this, probably, purgatory.
We have this old dog,
custodian of an ancient race of frogs,
doing what he knows how to do
and we too, taking and letting go,
that same story.

—Maxine Kumin

THE HOUSE-DOG'S GRAVE

(Haig, an English bulldog)

I've changed my ways a little: I cannot now
Run with you in the evenings along the shore,
Except in a kind of dream: and you, if you dream a moment,
You see me there.

So leave awhile the paw-marks on the front door
Where I used to scratch to go out or in,
And you'd soon open; leave on the kitchen floor
The marks of my drinking pan.

I cannot lie by your fire as I used to do
On the warm stone,
Nor at the foot of your bed: no, all the nights through
I lie alone.

But your kind thought has laid me less than six feet
Outside your window where firelight so often plays,
And where you sit to read—and I fear often grieving for me—
Every night your lamplight lies on my place.

You, man and woman, live so long it is hard
To think of you ever dying.
A little dog would get tired living so long.
I hope that when you are lying

Under the ground like me your lives will appear
As good and joyful as mine.
No, dears, that's too much hope: you are not so well cared for
As I have been,

And never have known the passionate undivided
Fidelities that I knew.
Your minds are perhaps too active, too many-sided. . . .
But to me you were true.

You were never masters, but friends. I was your friend.
I loved you well, and was loved. Deep love endures
To the end and far past the end. If this is my end,
I am not lonely. I am not afraid. I am still yours.

—Robinson Jeffers

Credits

Acknowledgments

My thanks to the following dogs and their owners:

Bonnie (aka Papa Wren's BonBon) (jacket):
Lisa, Neil, Anna, and Bennett Rofsky
Mozart (p. ii): Margaret Mintz & John Birdsall
Sparky (pp. v & 2): Sarah Longacre
Satyagraha (p. vi): Marystephanie Corsones &
Avery L. Smith
Birch (p. viii): Michael & Helene Campbell
Savannah (p. 5): Victoria Semproni
Güili (aka Willy) (pp. 6 & 7): Brook Davis Martínez
Pi (p. 8): Judith Ogus
Trasto (p. 11): Francisco J. Bermúdez
Stella (pp. 12 & 15): Ken & Isaac Krabbenhoft
Stray dog in Chinchón, Spain (p. 17)
Onyx (p. 18): the Jury family
Jezebel (p. 20): Steve Caumartin & Karen Graham
Husker (p. 23): Jan Rose
Max (p. 24): the Maddow-Zimet family
Jake (p. 27): Amy Kahn
Cayenne Pepper (aka Delmar's Free Spirit)
(p. 28): Michael & Diana Maloney

Casey (p. 31): Denise Bane & Rebecca Williams
Nestor (p. 32): Jody Winer
Juno (p. 35): Diana Kurz
Scout (p. 37): Richard McCormick
Piper (aka Rose's Tartan Piper) (p. 39):
Heidi Racioppo
Fossey (p. 40): Elizabeth Brannon, Michael Platt,
& Henry Platt-Brannon
Scuttlebutt (p. 43): Fran Smulcheski & John Ginty
Mahli (p. 44): Neal, Sue, Nina, & Gabe Herman
Stray dog in Sigüenza, Spain (p. 47)
Luke (p. 48): Michael Shashoua & Miriam Zoll
D.D. (pp. 50 & 53): Jim Matthews, Vikki
Papadouka, Elizabeth Goren, & Michael Silverman
Bronco (p. 54): Diana & German Meneses-
Góngora
Koa Kalani (p. 57): John Pfeiffer
Daisy (p. 59): Brooks & Nan McNamara
Muttley (p. 60): Rebecca Williams & Denise Bane
Toto & Howard Lanser (p. 64)

And thanks also to my neighbor, Heidi Racioppo, for putting up with many complaints about her dog, Beamme Yup Scotty, who inspired the title of this book.

Thanks to my partners at Bulfinch Press and Little, Brown who make it so much fun to work in publishing: Chester Chomka, Lyndsay Hanchett, and Allison Kolbeck. And thanks to The Stinehour Press for their continued devotion to the craft of fine printing and to Dean Bornstein for his perfect design.

This book only came together because of a great Dane who works like a dog.
Many thanks to my editor, Karen Dane.

Book design by Dean Bornstein
Printed by The Stinehour Press, Lunenburg, Vermont
Bound by Acme Bookbinding, Charlestown, Massachusetts